Preschool Skills

Kerry

Colors, Shapes, Sizes and Numbers

This book provides fun practice in readiness skills for early learners. Appealing art engages the attention of children as they complete the carefully chosen activities. The activities, which have been designed to prepare children for school, provide practice in beginning math, visual skills, fine-motor skills, language, thinking skills, and more! Children will enjoy exploring concepts related to *Colors, Shapes, Sizes and Numbers* as they complete a variety of fun activities!

Skills in this book include:
Counting • Shapes • Sizes • Visual discrimination
Thinking skills • Colors • Classification
And more!

Written by **Marcia S. Gresko** and **Vicky Shiotsu**

Cover illustration by **Georgene Griffin**

Illustrated by **Katy Arnsteen, Susanne DeMarco, Georgene Griffin, Joyce John, Patty McCloskey,** and **Gerry Oliviera**

FS132906 Colors, Shapes, Sizes, and Numbers
All rights reserved—Printed in the U.S.A.
Copyright © 2000 Frank Schaffer Publications, Inc.
23740 Hawthorne Blvd.
Torrance, CA 90505

ISBN 0-7682-0384-8

Table of Contents
Skills & Concepts

More or Less?

Circle the group in each box that has more.

Circle the group in each box that has less.

Big and Small

Draw a line to the matching thing that is the same size.

How Many?

Color, cut out, and count. Put all the cards with one thing in a group. Put all the cards with two things in a group. Put all the cards with three things in a group.

FS132906 Colors, Shapes, Sizes, and Numbers

Name _____

Funny Clowns

Color the circles.

6

Choo! Choo!

Color the squares.

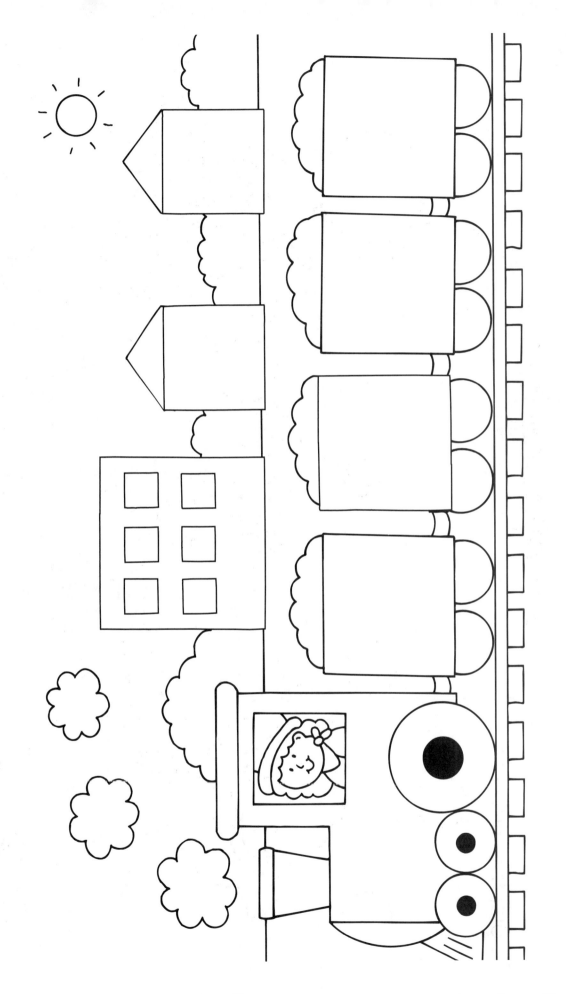

7

Name _____

Terrific Toys

Color the triangles.

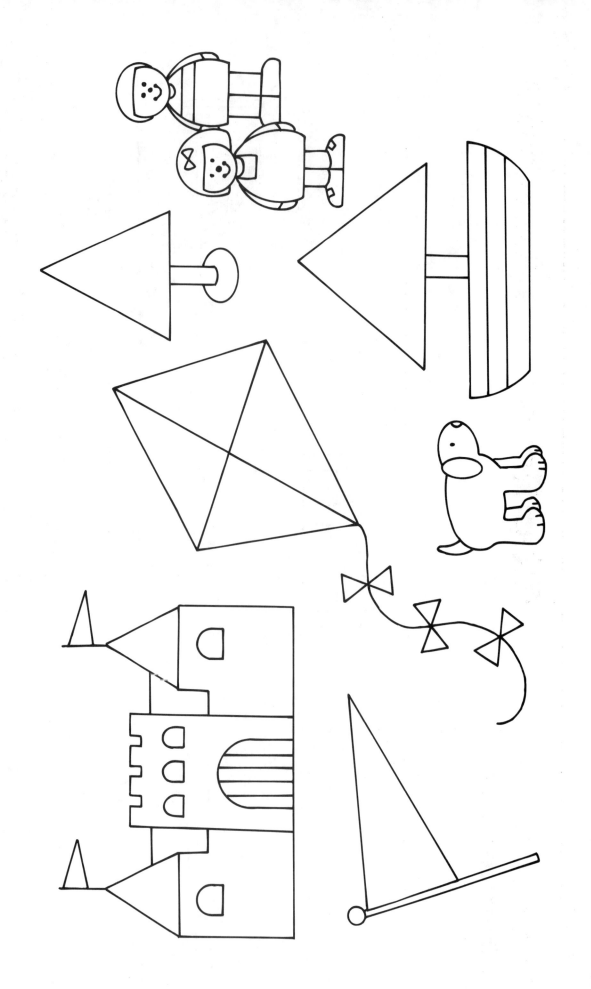

8

Name _____

Name

A Big House

Color the rectangles.

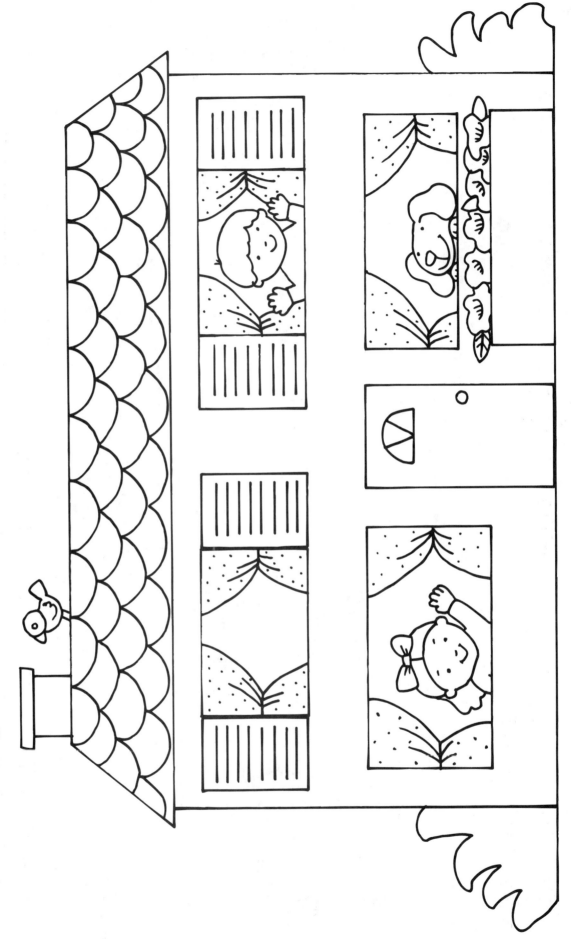

Time to Pack

Trace the color words.
Color the clothes for each child to match.

I Spy

Color and cut out.
Staple with page 12 to make a book.

I Spy

I spy with my little eye,
Something red,
Something sweet,
Something that is good to eat.

What is it?

1

I spy with my little eye,
Something yellow,
Something bright,
Something that shines at night.

What is it?

2

I spy with my little eye,
Something blue,
Something thick,
Something that goes tick, tick, tick.

What is it?

3

         FS132906 Colors, Shapes, Sizes, and Numbers

Name _____

I Spy

Color and cut out.
Staple with page 11 to make a book.

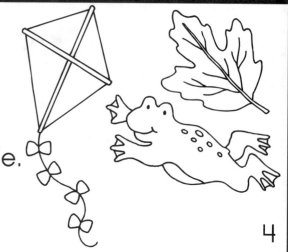

I spy with my little eye,
Something green,
Something wide,
Something that you fly outside.

What is it?

4

I spy with my little eye,
Something orange,
Something tiny,
Something that is very shiny.

What is it?

5

I spy with my little eye,
Something purple,
Something round,
Something that can roll around.

What is it?

6

12   FS132906 Colors, Shapes, Sizes, and Numbers

Name

Colorful Beads

Color the beads. Finish each pattern.

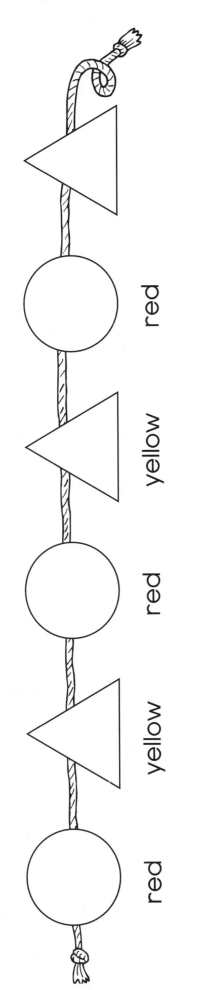

red   yellow   red   yellow   red

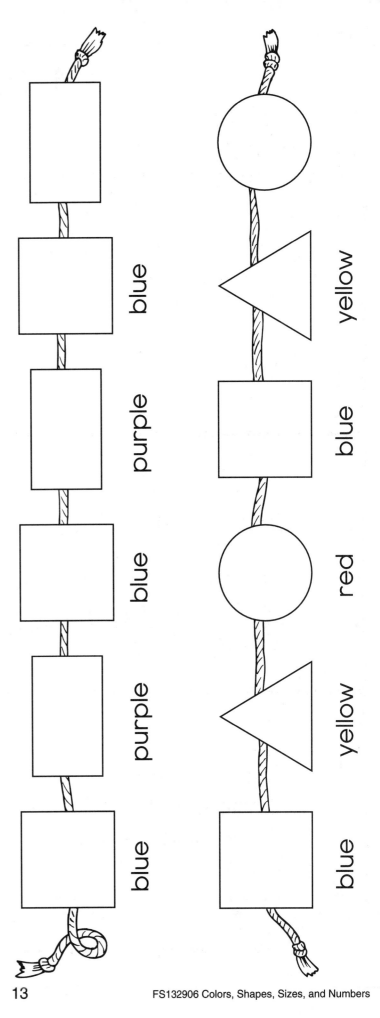

blue   purple   blue   purple   blue

yellow   blue   red   yellow   blue

FS132906 Colors, Shapes, Sizes, and Numbers

Building With Shapes

Color and cut out the shapes.
Use this page with page 15.
Use your cut-out shapes to make the pictures.

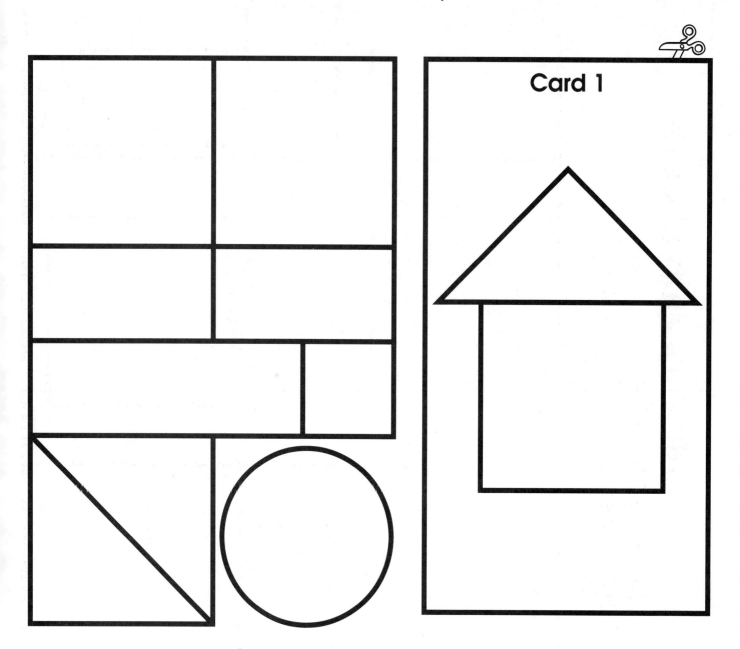

Teacher: Have the children first color and cut out the nine shapes and the pattern cards found on this page and the following page. Have the students identify each shape. Then have them begin with pattern card 1. Have the students copy the pattern by laying the shape pieces directly onto the pattern card. For an extra challenge, let the students copy the shape next to the pattern card. Afterwards, let the students create their own patterns with the shapes.

Name

Building With Shapes

Use this page with page 14.
Use your cut-out shapes to make the pictures.

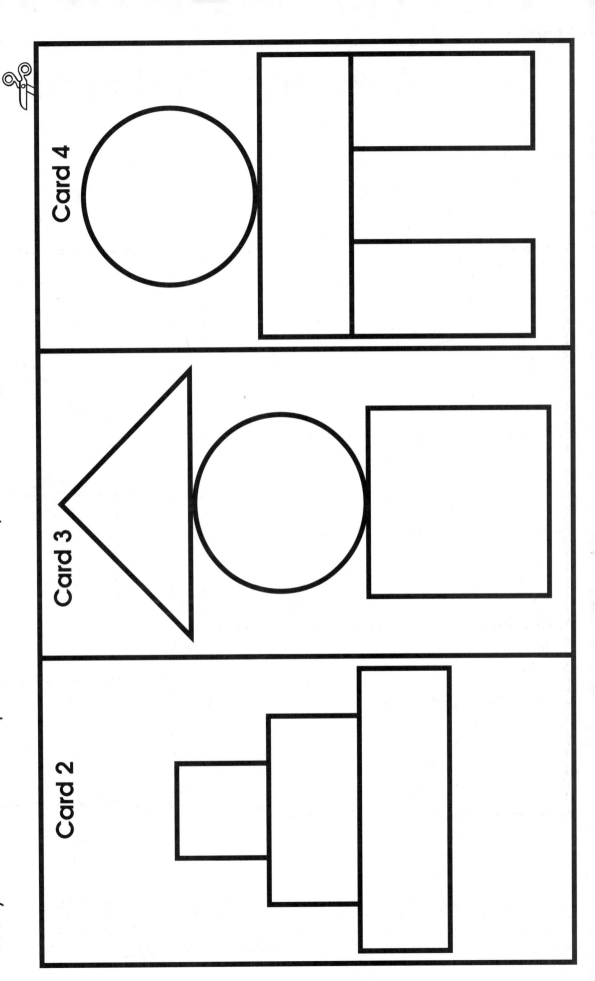

Can You Find These?

Find and color.

16

FS132906 Colors, Shapes, Sizes, and Numbers

Name _____

Big and Little

Trace the words. Color the big things red. Color the little things blue.

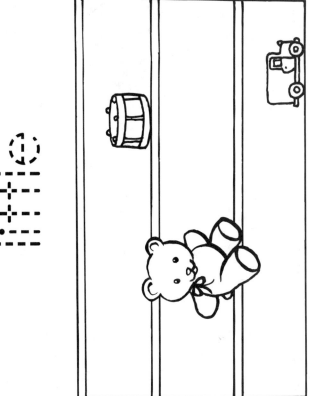

17

Name _____

Long and Short

Trace the words. Color the short things green. Color the long things orange.

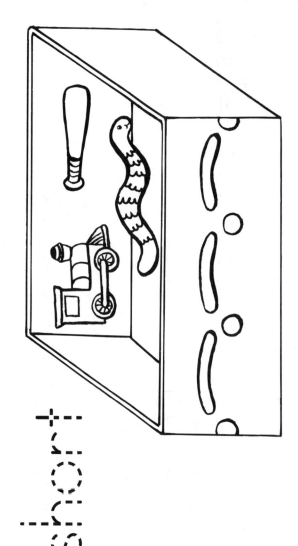

short

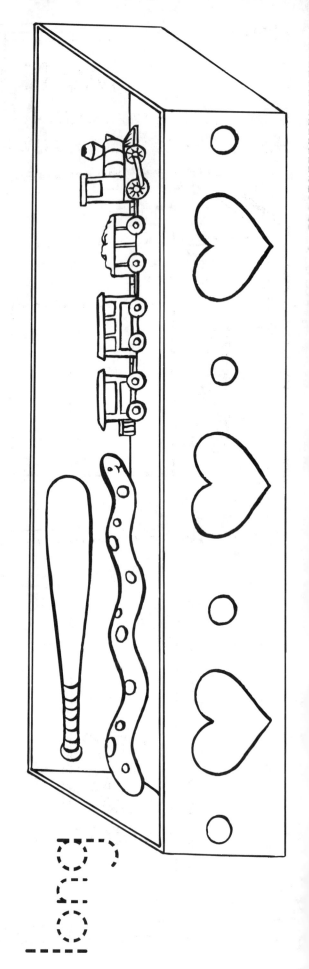

long

18

My Numbers Blocks

Cut, match, and paste. Use this page with page 20.
Paste the blocks to a piece of paper.

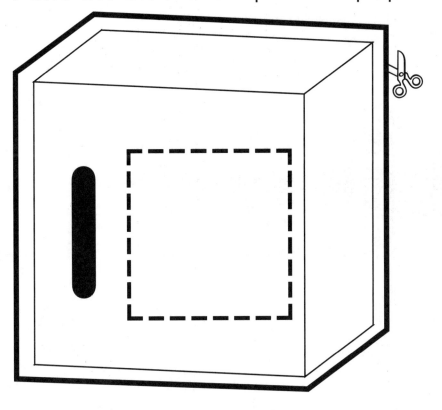

My Numbers Blocks

Cut, match, and paste. Use this page with page 19.
Paste the blocks to a piece of paper.

Name _____

A Color Game

Color the spaces. Play a game.

Start	green	red	blue	yellow	orange
					brown
red	brown	green	purple	white	black
black					
yellow	orange	white	green	blue	Finish

Teacher: To play this game, have students work in pairs and give each pair one copy of this page. Have them color the gameboard and cut out the markers. Next have them label 20 small pieces of paper 1 or 2, and put them in a paper bag. Then they take turns drawing a piece of paper from the bag, moving the markers one or two spaces depending on the number on the piece of paper, and naming the color they have landed on. The first one to get from Start to Finish wins.

21

FS132906 Colors, Shapes, Sizes, and Numbers

Name _____

People on the Move

Find and color these shapes: triangle, rectangle, oval, and square.

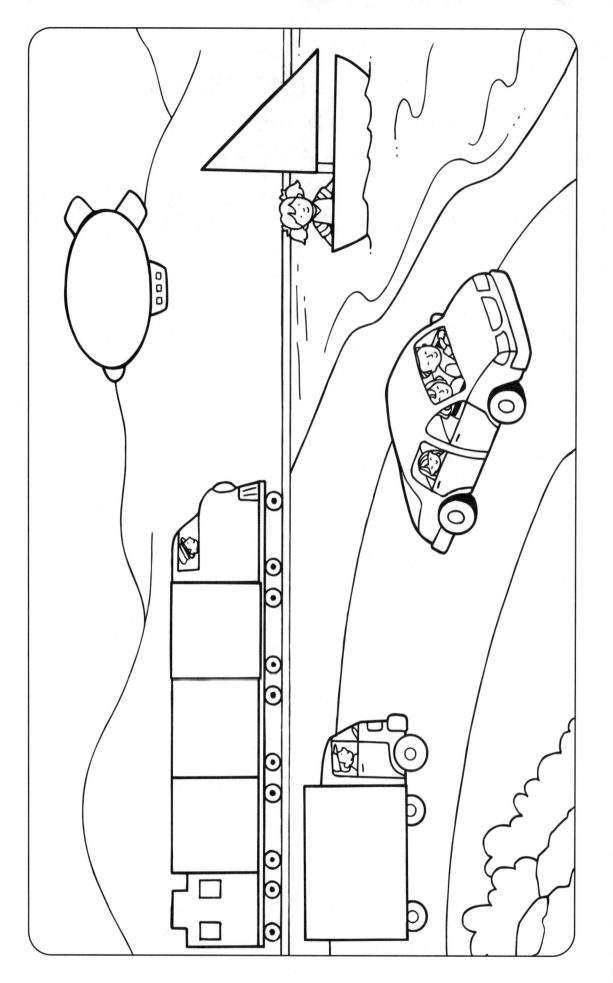

22

FS132906 Colors, Shapes, Sizes, and Numbers

In the Town

Count and write.

 ___ kids

 ___ buses

 ___ cars

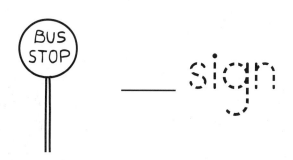 ___ sign

FS132906 Colors, Shapes, Sizes, and Numbers

All Kinds of Signs

Color the signs that are in the picture.

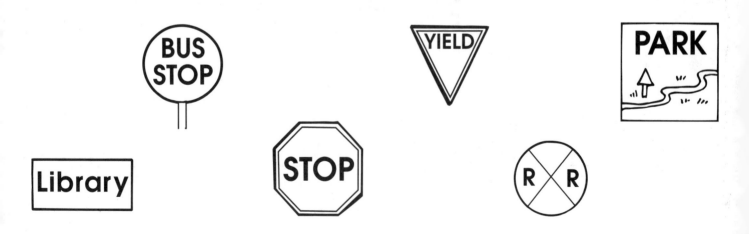

Colorful Cars

Color and cut out the cars. Then use them to make groups.
You can group them by color or by kind of car.

red	yellow	red
yellow	blue	blue
red	blue	yellow

Lots of Toys

Count. Draw a line to the number.

   **3**

    **2**

   **5**

      **1**

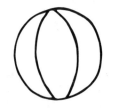 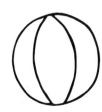 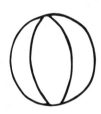 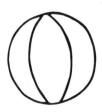 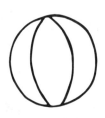   **4**

FS132906 Colors, Shapes, Sizes, and Numbers

Looking at Toys

Color the big toys red. Color the little toys blue.
Color the medium-sized toys yellow.

FS132906 Colors, Shapes, Sizes, and Numbers

Name _____

Finding Shapes

Color the triangles.

Color the squares.

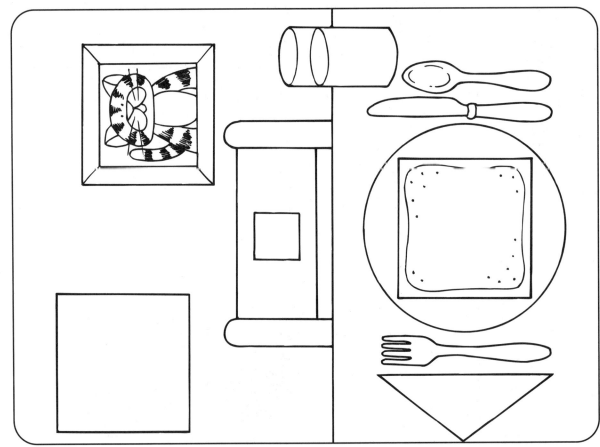

28

FS132906 Colors, Shapes, Sizes, and Numbers

Name _____

Finding More Shapes

Color the rectangles.

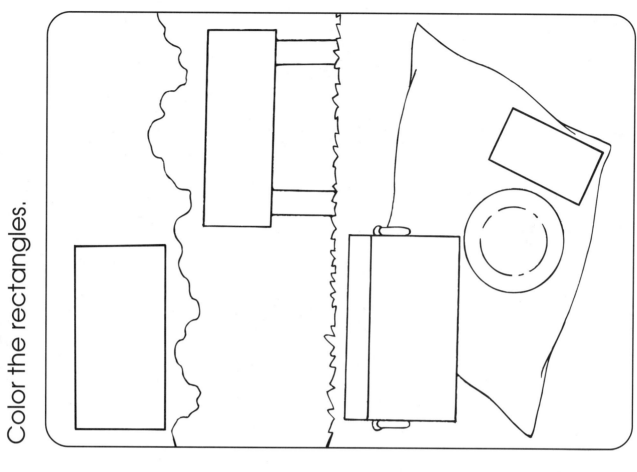

Color the circles.

FS132906 Colors, Shapes, Sizes, and Numbers

Name _____

Numbers Are Me!

Listen to your teacher read the rhyme.
Join in and say the rhyme with your teacher.

Two  ears to hear.

Two  feet to walk.

One 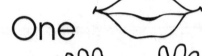 nose to smell.

One  mouth to talk.

Two  hands to touch.

Two eyes to see.

One  head to nod.

One special ME!

Name _____

Four at the Store

Count. Circle the number.

Find the Numbers

Find and color.

1 2 3 4 5

         FS132906 Colors, Shapes, Sizes, and Numbers